C++

Damien Loison

Terse & Good©

# C++ 11 & 14 Tips

by Damien Loison

Copyright @ 2016 Damien Loison. All rights reserved.

Terse & Good publishing Company
54 Upwood road, SE 12 8AN, London, UK
http://www.TerseAndGood.com/index.html
contacts@TerseAndGood.com

The information in this book is distributed on an "As is" basis, without warranty. While every precaution has been taken in the preparation of this book, neither the author nor the publisher shall have any liability to any person or entity with respect to any loss or damage caused or alleged to be caused directly or indirectly by the instructions contained in this book. If any code samples or other technology this work contains or describes is subject to open source licences or the intellectual property rights of others, it is your responsibility to ensure that your use thereof complies with such licences and/or rights

# 1. Contents

1. Contents ........................................................................................................................... 1
2. Introduction ..................................................................................................................... 5
3. Data member initializer ................................................................................................... 6
4. Initializer list .................................................................................................................... 7
   A. Create ........................................................................................................................ 7
   B. Initialize vector .......................................................................................................... 7
   C. Initialize classes ......................................................................................................... 7
5. Raw string literals ............................................................................................................ 9
6. auto ............................................................................................................................... 10
7. decltype ......................................................................................................................... 11
   A. General .................................................................................................................... 11
   B. Template .................................................................................................................. 11
8. Range for ....................................................................................................................... 13
9. Alias using versus typedef ............................................................................................. 14
10. Class function keywords .............................................................................................. 15
    A. delete ...................................................................................................................... 15
    B. final ......................................................................................................................... 15
    C. override ................................................................................................................... 16
    D. default ..................................................................................................................... 16
11. Delegating constructor ................................................................................................ 18
12. Inherited constructor ................................................................................................... 19
13. Move semantics: lvalue, rvalue, and std::move .......................................................... 20
    A. lvalue and rvalue and references ........................................................................... 20
    B. overloading and std::move ..................................................................................... 21
14. Move semantics: Move constructor and move assignment operator ........................ 22
15. Move semantics: implicit member functions created by the compiler ...................... 25
16. Move semantics: Move operator and constructor for std::vector .............................. 27
17. Move semantics: perfect forwarding ........................................................................... 29
    A. Answer .................................................................................................................... 29

  B. Explanations ................................................................................................................ 30

17. Move semantics: Differences between std::move and std::forward .............................. 32

19. Vector and map 'emplace' ............................................................................................. 34

20. std::array ......................................................................................................................... 35

21. Hash container ................................................................................................................ 36

  A. Using default hash functions ..................................................................................... 36

  B. Define your own hash function ................................................................................. 37

22. std:tuple .......................................................................................................................... 39

  A. Example ...................................................................................................................... 39

  B. Unpack tuple result with std::tie ................................................................................ 39

23. External template ............................................................................................................ 40

24. nullptr .............................................................................................................................. 42

25. lambda ............................................................................................................................. 44

  A. lambda in another function ...................................................................................... 44

  B. lambda using an external variable ............................................................................ 44

  C. Specify the return type .............................................................................................. 45

  D. Using lambda in std::algorithm .................................................................................. 45

  E. lamda in functionsignature ........................................................................................ 45

  F. lamda with dangling reference .................................................................................. 46

26. std::function<...> ............................................................................................................ 47

27. Smart pointers: std::shared_ptr ...................................................................................... 48

  A. std::make_shared ...................................................................................................... 48

  B. Using custom deleter ................................................................................................. 48

28. Smart pointers: std:unique_ptr ....................................................................................... 49

  A. Move ........................................................................................................................... 49

  B. Using custom deleter ................................................................................................. 49

  C. Pimpl ........................................................................................................................... 49

29. Smart pointers: std::weak_ptr ........................................................................................ 51

30. Enum ................................................................................................................................ 52

31. long long .......................................................................................................................... 53

32. cstdint: sized integer ....................................................................................................... 55

33. static_assert ............................................................................................................... 57
34. Variadic template ..................................................................................................... 58
35. Exceptions ................................................................................................................ 59
   A. std::exception .................................................................................................... 59
   B. noexcept ............................................................................................................ 59
   C. noexcept operator ............................................................................................ 60
36. Time utilities ............................................................................................................. 61
37. Random generator ................................................................................................... 62
38. Regular expressions ................................................................................................. 63
39. User-defined literals ................................................................................................. 65
40. constexpr .................................................................................................................. 66
41. Union ........................................................................................................................ 67
42. Attribute ................................................................................................................... 68
43. std::algorithm ........................................................................................................... 69
   A. minmax_element ............................................................................................... 69
   B. std::all_of, std::any_of, std::none_of ................................................................. 69
   C. std::is_sorted .................................................................................................... 70
   D. std::count, count_if .......................................................................................... 70
   E. std::find, find_if ................................................................................................ 71
   F. std::copy_if ....................................................................................................... 71
   G. std::iota, std::generate .................................................................................... 72
   H. std::transform ................................................................................................... 73
44. std::bind ................................................................................................................... 74
45. Concurrency: std::async ........................................................................................... 76
   A. Example ............................................................................................................. 76
   B. Options: deferred .............................................................................................. 77
46. Concurrency: std::atomic ......................................................................................... 79
47. Concurrency: Mutex ................................................................................................. 81
   A. Example ............................................................................................................. 81
   B. Defer + try_lock ................................................................................................ 82
48. Concurrency: Multithread condition variables ....................................................... 83

1. Contents                                                                                                                   3

| | A. | Simple example | 83 |
|---|---|---|---|
| | B. | Spurious wakeup | 85 |
| 49. | | Index | 88 |

# 2. Introduction

Terse and good.

- You are an experienced C++ programmer
- You want to know the novelties in the C++ 11 and C++ 14
- You want working examples without the verbiage
- You do not want a reference book. If you need one http://en.cppreference.com/w/

What you need:

- Visual Studio: at least 2013 but 2015 is better
  https://blogs.msdn.microsoft.com/vcblog/2015/06/19/c111417-features-in-vs-2015-rtm/
- Gcc: better to use at least 4.8 for C++ 11 and 5. for C++ 14. See
  https://gcc.gnu.org/projects/cxx-status.html#cxx11 and
  https://gcc.gnu.org/projects/cxx-status.html#cxx14
- Clang: at least 3.4 http://clang.llvm.org/cxx_status.html

# 3. Data member initializer

You can now initialize non static member variables directly without going through the constructor. Very nice when you have several constructors:

```cpp
struct C11
{
    int m_a = 10;
    int m_b = 30;

    C11() {}                     // m_a=10, m_b=30
    C11(int b_): m_b(b_) {}      // m_a=10, m_b=b_

};
```

# 4. Initializer list

## A. Create

You can create an initializer list using std::initializer_list. The list has only three methods: size(), begin(), end(). With it, you can initialize vectors, maps or classes

```cpp
#include <initializer_list>
#include <iostream>

std::initializer_list<int> list = { 1,2,3,4,5 };

std::cout << "size = " << list.size() << std::endl;

// all values with range for loop
for (auto val : list)
{
    std::cout << val << "-";
}
std::cout << std::endl;

// all values with standard loop
for (auto iter = list.begin(); iter != list.end(); ++iter)
{
    std::cout << *iter << "_";
}
std::cout << std::endl;
```

The output is:

```
size = 5
1-2-3-4-5-
1_2_3_4_5_
```

## B. Initialize vector

and map

```cpp
std::vector<int> vec = { 1,2,3,4,5 };

std::vector<std::vector<int>> vec_vec = { { 1,2,3,4,5 },{34} };

std::map<std::string, int> map1 = { { "a",1 } ,{ "b",2 } ,{ "c",3 } };
```

## C. Initialize classes

You can initialize classes or struct

4. Initializer list 7

```cpp
struct C11
{
    int m_a;
    double m_b;
    C11(int a_, double b_): m_a(a_), m_b(b_) {}
};

C11 c11 = { 1, 2.4 };
```

However, be aware that a constructor with initializer list always has the priority:

```cpp
struct C11
{
    int m_a;
    double m_b;
    C11(int a_, double b_): m_a(a_), m_b(b_) {}
    C11(const std::initializer_list<int>& list_) {}
};

// error: 2.4 is not an integer to convert to
// std::initializer_list<int>
C11 c11 = { 1, 2.4 };
```

Lastly, if no constructor is defined, you can initialize the member variables directly with the initializer list. Please note: you can't change the order of the member variables inside the class without breaking the interface.

```cpp
struct C11
{
    int m_a;
    double m_b;
};

// m_a = 1, m_b = 2.4
C11 c11 = { 1, 2.4 };
```

# 5. Raw string literals

Python "style" to be able to have '\' (backslash) and '"' (quote) without using '\'. We use R"(...)":

```
std::cout << R"(a b   t   d   )" << std::endl; // a b   t   d
std::cout << R"(a b \t "d" )" << std::endl; // a b \t "d"
```

the only problem appears when having a ')"' at the end of the chain of characters. In this case you can use, for example: R"__(...)__" or R"***(...)***"

```
std::cout << R"__(a b \t "d" )__" << std::endl; // a b \t "d"
std::cout << R"__(a b \t "d" )")__" << std::endl; // a b \t "d" )"
```

# 6. auto

Auto follows the same rules as template parameters deduction. Particularly it will not match *const* or references. These have to be specified explicitly. Usually we use it to avoid lengthy declaration or in template. Examples:

```cpp
#include <map>

int main()
{
    // int a = 3
    auto a = 3;

    // unsigned int a_unsigned = 4;
    auto a_unsigned = 4u;

    // int& a_ref = a
    auto& a_ref = a;

    // const int& a_ref = a
    const auto& a_const_ref = a;

    // lenghty declaration
    std::map<std::string, std::double_t> map1;
    auto iter = map1.cbegin();

    return 0;
}
```

For template example, see decltype item 7.B

# 7. decltype

*decltype*, declare type, is mainly used for template.

## A. General

We get the type of a variable and we use it to declare another variable or expression. The syntax is *decltype(...)*. If you want to declare a reference you need to use *decltype((...))*:

```cpp
// decltype(i1) = int
// int integer = 4;
decltype(i1) integer = 4;

// decltype((i1)) = int&
// int& reference = i1;
decltype((i1)) reference = i1;
```

## B. Template

Overloading function with different output type

```cpp
// function taking an integer and returning a reference
int& fc_overload(int& i_) { return i_; }

// function taking a double and returning a copy
double fc_overload(double& d_) { return d_+3.; }

// this template will call either one or the other fc_overload
// return type of fc_overload using '->decltype(fc_overload(...))'
// C11 style
template <typename T>
auto function(T& t_) -> decltype(fc_overload(t_))
{
    return fc_overload(t_);
}

int main()
{
    // template function for integer
    //   decltype(fc_overload(i_)) = int&
    int i1 = 3;
    int& i2 = function(i1);

    // template function for double
    //   decltype(fc_overload(d_)) = double
    double d1 = 3.;
    double d2 = function(d1);
```

```
        return 0;
    }
```

In C++ 14, the function is even simpler:

```
    // C14 style
    template <typename T>
    decltype(auto) function(T& t_)
    {
        return fc_overload(t_);
    }
```

# 8. Range for

Iterate through a collection.

```cpp
#include <iostream>
#include <map>
#include <vector>
#include <string>

int main()
{
    // range for for vector
    std::vector<int> vec = { 1,2,3,4,5 };
    for (const int& val : vec)
        std::cout << val << " - ";
    std::cout << std::endl << std::endl;

    // range for for map
    std::map<std::string, int> map1 = { { "a",1 } ,{ "b",2 } ,{ "c",3 } };
    for (const auto& pair1 : map1)
        std::cout << pair1.first << " - " << pair1.second << std::endl;

    return 0;
}
```

and the output is

```
1 - 2 - 3 - 4 - 5 -

a - 1
b - 2
c - 3
```

# 9. Alias using versus typedef

Alias *using* is similar to *typedef* with two main improvements

- Alias can be templatized
- More intuitive declaration

The second point can be understood quickly:

```cpp
// map
typedef std::map<std::string, int> C98Map;
using    C11Map = std::map<std::string, int>;

// pointer of function
typedef  int(*C98Function)(double);
using    C11Function = int(*)(double);
```

The first point is more powerful: we can use alias with template. For example:

```cpp
template <typename T>
using    C11Map = std::map<std::string, T>;

C11Map<int> map;
```

# 10. Class function keywords

## A.   delete

If you want to remove a signature automatically created by C++ (like copy constructor, assignment operator, …) just declare it *delete*. Useful for some patterns (singleton, non-copyable class, …)

```cpp
struct C11
{
    C11() {}
    // no copy allowed
    C11(const C11&) = delete;
};

int main()
{
    C11 c11;

    // error C2280: 'C11::C11(const C11 &)':
    // attempting to reference a deleted function
    C11 c11_copy(c11);

    return 0;
}
```

## B.   final

A function declared as final cannot be overridden by derived classes

```cpp
struct C11
{
    virtual void f_final(const int&) final {}
};

struct C11_Derived : public C11
{
    // error: function declared as 'final'
    // cannot be overridden
    virtual void f_final(const int&) {}
};
```

## C. override

The override keyword specifies that the current function is an override of a function defined in a base class. In this way you can avoid mistakes due to different signatures when you think you override a function but indeed create one:

```cpp
struct C11
{
            void f_non_virtual() {}
    virtual void f_virtual() {}
    virtual void f_const() const {}
    virtual void f_const_int(const int&) {}
    virtual void f_final(const int&) final {}
};

struct C11_Derived : public C11
{
            void f_non_virtual() override {} // error non virtual
    virtual void f_virtual() override {} // OK
    virtual void f_const() override {} // error non const
    virtual void f_const_int(const double&) override {} // error different signature
    virtual void f_final(const int&) override {} // error final
};
```

## D. default

Before C++ 11 , the compiler automatically generated four member functions, even if you did not declare them yourself: constructor, copy constructor, assignment operator, and destructor (add the address operator if you are a purist). C++ 11 introduced two new operators: move constructor and move assignment operator (item 14). However, to avoid inconsistency between the operators and for backward compatibility, it does not generate the move operators if a destructor, copy operator, or copy constructor are defined. Similarly it does not create them if a move operator is defined. Therefore, this code will fail to compile

```cpp
struct C11
{
    C11() {}
    // move constructor
    C11(const C11&& c11_) {}
};

C11 c11;
// error here: no copy constructor is defined:
C11 c12(c11);
```

We will have to declare the copy constructor. If we want the default one just specify it by using the keyword '*default*':

```cpp
struct C11
{
    C11() {}
    // move constructor
    C11(const C11&& c11_) {}
    // default copy constructor
    C11(const C11& c11_) = default;
};
```

Similarly, if we want that the compiler to define the move constructor (useful, for example, with *std::vector*, see item 16) we have to define it explicitly or using the default implementation. Otherwise the copy constructor will be used and this could have a performance issue

```cpp
struct C11
{
    C11() {}
    // default move constructor
    C11(const C11&& c11_) = default
    // copy constructor
    C11(const C11& c11_) {}
};
```

# 11. Delegating constructor

C++11 allows you to call another constructor. The object will be created after the completion of the first constructor. No need of a helper function.

```cpp
struct C11
{
    int m_a;

    C11(int a_) : m_a(a_) {}
    C11() : C11(3) {} // OK
};
```

# 12. Inherited constructor

You can forward the constructor from the base class to the derived class:

```
struct C11
{
    C11()        { std::cout << "C11()" << std::endl; }
    C11(int a_) { std::cout << "C11(int a_)" << std::endl; }
};

struct C11_Derived : public C11
{
    using C11::C11;
};

C11_Derived c11;     // C11()
C11_Derived c12(3);  // C11(int a_)
```

You can also create a constructor in the derived class. However, be careful because it can quickly become a mess:

```
struct C11
{
    C11()        { std::cout << "C11()" << std::endl; }
    C11(int a_) { std::cout << "C11(int a_)" << std::endl; }
};

struct C11_Derived : public C11
{
    using C11::C11;
    C11_Derived(double b_) { std::cout << "C11_Derived(double b_)" << std::endl; }
};

int main()
{
    C11_Derived c12(3);   // C11(int a_)

    C11_Derived c13(3.);  // C11() + C11(double b_)

    return 0;
}
```

And the output is:

```
C11(int a_) // C11_Derived c12(3);
C11()       // C11_Derived c13(3.);
C11_Derived(double b_)
```

12. Inherited constructor                                                      19

# 13. Move semantics: lvalue, rvalue, and std::move

One of the most problematic features of C++ 99 and C++ 03 is their management of temporary variables. This could be a real problem of optimization as shown in the program below. First we must introduce the concepts of lvalue and rvalue.

## A.  lvalue and rvalue and references

To keep the explanation clear enough, I will define lvalue and rvalue loosely. What is important for us is lvalue and rvalue references.

In C, a *lvalue* is an expression that may appear on the left or on the right side of an assignment. For example

```cpp
int a = 3; // a is a lvalue
```

In C, a *rvalue* can only appear on the right side of an assignment. For example, the result of a function could be a temporary object:

```cpp
// a function returning a string by value
std::string fcRvalue() { return "rvalue"; }

// the function fcRvalue returns a temporary object rvalue
std::string lvalue = fcRvalue();
```

On the last line, C++ 03, without optimization, must call the copy constructor of the string class to create the lvalue from the rvalue returning from fcRvalue. In the string class this means to create a new array to store the string, and remove the old array in the rvalue. It would be very nice to be able to use the same array, i.e. to move the array to the new string. C++ 11 introduces therefore two new function: the move constructor and move operator (see it in item 14 and item 15). The concept of lvalue and rvalue in C++ is a little bit more complicated than in C, see example http://accu.org/index.php/journals/227. However, we can understand the move semantics with our "definitions". Note that *std::string* is already optimized in many compiler implementations.

We must introduce the concept of rvalue reference, denoted by *&&*. With the previous definition *fcRvalue()*, we can write

```cpp
// the function fcRvalue returns a temporary object rvalue
// we extend the life of the rvalue returned by f()
std::string&& rvalue = fcRvalue();
std::cout << rvalue << std::endl;
```

We must now understand the function overloading between lvalue and rvalue references and std::move

## B.     overloading and std::move

To create a signature for rvalue you need to add && to the type.

```cpp
void f(int&& i_) {…}
```

Then you can create two overloading functions with different signature for lvalue and rvalue:

```cpp
// lvalue signature
void f(int&  i_) { std::cout << "call f(lvalue)" << std::endl; }

// rvalue signature
void f(int&& i_) { std::cout << "call f(rvalue)" << std::endl; }

int main()
{
    // calling lvalue overloading function
    int lvalue = 0;
    f(lvalue);

    // 1. calling rvalue overloading function
    f(int(0));

    // 2. cast lvalue in rvalue
    // calling rvalue overloading function
    f(static_cast<int&&>(lvalue));

    // 3. std::move to cast lvalue in rvalue
    // calling rvalue overloading function
    f(std::move(lvalue));

    return 0;
}
```

The output of this program is:

```
call f(lvalue) // f(lvalue)
call f(rvalue) // f(int(0))
call f(rvalue) // f(static_cast<int&&>(lvalue))
call f(rvalue) // f(std::move(lvalue));
```

If you need to be able to cast a lvalue to a rvalue, it is better to use *std::move()* instead of casting it manually.

13. Move semantics: lvalue, rvalue, and std::move

# 14. Move semantics: Move constructor and move assignment operator

We can use overloading lvalue and rvalue features to improve the efficiency of our classes when we deal with copy from rvalue. If our class has some pointers to memory, it is more efficient to move them instead of creating a new one. We define the move constructor and move assignment operator using the symbol **&&** to express that the input is a rvalue and can be "moved". The signature for the move constructor will be (for a C11 class):

```
C11(C11&&) { …}
```

In the following example the class owns a pointer to an int and we define the move constructor:

```cpp
#include <iostream>

struct C11
{
    // ressource we want to move
    int* m_intPtr = nullptr;

    C11(int a_) : m_intPtr(new int(a_)) {
        std::cout << "constructor" << std::endl;
    }

    // copy constructor: create new array
    C11(const C11& c11_) : m_intPtr(new int(*c11_.m_intPtr)) {
        std::cout << "copy constructor" << std::endl;
    }

    // move constructor : reuse the array
    // note that the rvalue is not constant
    C11(C11&& c11_) : m_intPtr(c11_.m_intPtr) {
        c11_.m_intPtr = nullptr;
        std::cout << "move constructor" << std::endl;
    }

    // destructor
    ~C11() {
        delete m_intPtr;
        std::cout << "destructor" << std::endl;
    }
};

// Create a local variable and return by value
C11 f()
{
    std::cout << "enter f()" << std::endl;
```

```
        C11 c11(2); // local variable
        std::cout << "end creation local c11 in f()" << std::endl;

        return c11;
    }

    int main()
    {
        // the function f() returns a temporary object rvalue
        C11 c11 = f();

        std::cout << "end creation local c11 in main()" << std::endl;

        return 0;
    }
```

The output is:

```
enter f()
constructor // local variable in f()
end creation local c11 in f()
move constructor // C11 c11 = f();
destructor // destructor temporary variable from return f()
end creation local c11 in main()
destructor // destructor local variable in main()
```

The move operator is called to move the temporary variable from f(). After moving it, the **destructor** is called for this temporary variable. Therefore, we need to set up the pointer to nullptr for the temporary variable in the move constructor

```
c11_.m_intPtr = nullptr;
```

Without the move constructor, the copy constructor would be called and a new array would be created and populated with a copy of the old array. Then the old array would be removed.

Our example are compiled in debug mode without optimization. If we compile in Release mode, the compiler is authorized to optimize the rvalue to remove it completely. Below is the output in release mode. No more move constructor and destructor.

```
enter f()
constructor
end creation local c11 in f()
end creation local c11 in main()
destructor
```

This example is very simple and can be optimized quite easily by the compiler. Usually it is not the case and the move operator is very useful.

If we have class member variable with a move function constructor, like *std::string*, we need to tell the compiler we would like to use the move constructor instead of the copy constructor. For that we need to use std::move as shown in item 13.B

14. Move semantics: Move constructor and move assignment operator                                    23

```cpp
struct C11
{
    std::string m_string;
    // use move constructor from std::string class
    C11(C11&& c11_) : m_string(std::move(c11_.m_string))// move constructor
    {
    }
};
```

Note that the default move constructor and move assignment operator will call *std::move* on each member

# 15. Move semantics: implicit member functions created by the compiler

When creating an empty class, C++ 11 defines two new implicit functions in addition to the standard ones: move constructor and operator. Therefore, we have now six implicit functions:

- Default constructor
- Copy constructor
- Copy assignment operator
- Destructor
- Move constructor
- Move assignment operator

If you do not define a move constructor, the copy constructor will be used. For example, in the program below with both copy and move constructors, the move constructor is used:

```cpp
#include <iostream>

// helper function
void print(char * str_) { std::cout << str_ << std::endl; }

// class with a copy and move constructors defined,
struct C11
{
    C11(                ) { print("         constructor"); }
    C11(const C11&  c11_) { print("copy     constructor"); }
    C11(      C11&& c11_) { print("move     constructor"); }
};


// Create a local variable and return by value
C11 f() { C11 c11; return c11; }

int main()
{

    // the function f() returns a temporary object rvalue
    // the move constructor is used
    C11 c11 = f();

    return 0;
}
```

Output:

```
         constructor
move     constructor
```

but if we remove the move constructor:

```
// C11(const C11&& c11_) { print("move constructor"); }
```

And we get the output:

```
        constructor
copy constructor
```

Similarly, if we define a move constructor without defining the copy constructor, the compiler will not generate the copy constructor. If we want the compiler to generate it for us, we have to use the *default* keyword. See item 10.D.

```
struct C11
{
    C11(                  ) { print("       constructor"); }
    C11(const C11&  c11_) = default;
    C11(      C11&& c11_) { print("move constructor"); }
};
```

# 16. Move semantics: Move operator and constructor for std::vector

The objective of the move operators is avoiding paying the cost associated to copy the resources if we do not need to. In the program below we show the result when the size of the vector increase and the array of objects has to be moved from one location to the other. The move constructor is used (we will see in item 19 that it is better to use *emplace_back* instead of *push_back*).

```cpp
#include <iostream>
#include <string>
#include <vector>

void print(const std::string& str_) { std::cout << str_ << std::endl; }

struct C11
{
    C11(int a_) { print("constructor"); }
    C11(const C11& c11_) { print("copy constructor"); }
    C11(C11&& c11_) { print("move constructor"); }
    ~C11() { print("destructor"); }
};

int main()
{
    // on windows
    std::vector<C11> vec;
    print("-- vec.push_back(1) --------------");
    vec.push_back(1);
    print("-- vec.push_back(2) --------------");
    vec.push_back(2);
    print("-- vec.push_back(3) --------------");
    vec.push_back(3);
    print("-- exit -----------------------------");

    return 0;
}
```

And the output is:

```
-- vec.push_back(1) --------------
Constructor // create temporary variable C(1)
move constructor // move temporary variable into vec[0]
destructor // remove temporary variable
-- vec.push_back(2) --------------
Constructor // create temporary variable C(2)
            // increase capacity from 1->2
move constructor // move vec[0] into its new location
```

```
destructor    // remove old location vec[0]
move constructor // move temporary variable into vec[1]
destructor // remove temporary variable
-- vec.push_back(3) --------------
Constructor // create temporary variable C(3)
            // increase capacity from 2->3
```
**move constructor** `// move vec[0] into its new location`
**move constructor** `// move vec[1] into its new location`
```
destructor // remove old location vec[0]
destructor// remove old location vec[1]
move constructor // move temporary variable into vec[2]
destructor// remove temporary variable
-- exit ---------------------------
Destructor // remove vec[0]
Destructor // remove vec[1]
Destructor // remove vec[2]
```

When we increase the size of the vector, the vector class needs to allocate a bigger array in memory and move the existing objects in their new location. The move constructor is used. This is less costly than using the copy constructor. Note that the destructor is also called for the objects in their old location.

# 17. Move semantics: perfect forwarding

We have the two functions of item 13.B:

```cpp
// lvalue signature
void f(int&  i_) { std::cout << "call f(lvalue)" << std::endl; }

// rvalue signature
void f(int&& i_) { std::cout << "call f(rvalue)" << std::endl; }
```

and we want to create a template function which call the correct function if the argument is either a lvalue or a rvalue. The problem is not trivial. Before explaining the solution, we give the answer.

## A.   Answer

In the program below. Look at *f_perfectForwarding*:

```cpp
#include <iostream>
#include <string>
#include <vector>

void print(const std::string& str_) { std::cout << str_ << std::endl; }

// lvalue signature
void f(int&  i_) { std::cout << "call f(lvalue)" << std::endl; }

// rvalue signature
void f(int&& i_) { std::cout << "call f(rvalue)" << std::endl; }

// perfect forwarding
// call f(int&   i_) for lvalue
// call f(int&&  i_) for rvalue
template <typename T>
void f_perfectForwarding(T&& t_)
{
    f(std::forward<T>(t_));
}

int main()
{
    // calling lvalue overloading function
    int lvalue = 0;
    f_perfectForwarding(lvalue);

    // 1. calling rvalue overloading function
    f_perfectForwarding(int(0));
```

```
        // 2. cast lvalue in rvalue
        // calling rvalue overloading function
        f_perfectForwarding(static_cast<int&&>(lvalue));

        // 3. std::move to cast lvalue in rvalue
        // calling rvalue overloading function
        f_perfectForwarding(std::move(lvalue));

        return 0;
    }
```

And the output is, as expected:

```
    call f(lvalue)
    call f(rvalue)
    call f(rvalue)
    call f(rvalue)
```

## B.  Explanations

Before coming with the final solution we could think of several possibilities:

First, we could try to use references:

```
    template <typename T>
    void f_perfectForwarding(T& t_) { f(t_); }
```

Unfortunately we can't even compile because of

```
    // cannot convert argument 1 from 'int' to 'int &'
    f_perfectForwarding(int(0));
```

Therefore, we replace the & by && to accept the rvalue and with the knowledge of the collapsing rules for ***template** T&&* are :

- T is lvalue reference  && => lvalue reference
- T is rvalue reference  && => rvalue reference

Or, in a more standard form:

- &    && => &
- &&   && => &&

The function becomes:

```
    template <typename T>
    void f_perfectForwarding(T&& t_) { f(t_); }
```

The problem is that we call only the lvalue function f when calling **f(t_)**. The output is:

```
call f(lvalue) // OK
call f(lvalue) // instead of rvalue
call f(lvalue) // instead of rvalue
call f(lvalue) // instead of rvalue
```

The reason is that the compiler must interpret **t_** as a lvalue. Indeed, consider the code:

```
template <typename T>
void f_perfectForwarding(T&& t_)
{
    f(t_);
    f(t_);
}
```

If **t_** in the first call is considered as a rvalue, the function f() could move **t_**, for example, for a vector class, move the array to a new vector, and the second call could fail. Therefore, the compiler has to consider **t_** as lvalue. We need a way to create a rvalue if it is a rvalue, but keep the lvalue as it is. The solution is to cast it with the collapsing rule as before

```
template <typename T>
void f_perfectForwarding(T&& t_)
{
    f(static_cast<T&&>(t_));
}
```

This works fine. The *std::forward* is just a refinement of the *template static_cast<T&&>*.

# 18. Move semantics: Differences between std::move and std::forward

In the program of item 17.A, in main, we have shown that *std::move* is only a *static_cast<...&&>*

```
// 2. cast lvalue in rvalue
// calling rvalue overloading function
f_perfectForwarding(static_cast<int&&>(lvalue));

// 3. std::move to cast lvalue in rvalue
// calling rvalue overloading function
f_perfectForwarding(std::move(lvalue));
```

In this case *static_cast<int&&>(lvalue)* is indeed a rvalue.

But we have also shown in item 17.B that *std::forward* is also a *static_cast<...&&>*

```
template <typename T>
void f_perfectForwarding(T&& t_)
{
    f(static_cast<T&&>(t_));
}
```

In this case the *template static_cast<T&&>* gives a reference of lvalue if T is a lvalue, and a rvalue otherwise.

The difference between the two cast is the *template <typename T>*. For templates, the *T&&* has a different meaning than for defined type and is managed by the collapsing rules:

- T is lvalue reference && => lvalue reference
- T is rvalue reference && => rvalue reference

    Or, in a more standard form:

- &     && => &
- &&    && => &&

Which explains the difference of behaviour between *std::move* and *std::forward*.

We look now how the return is implemented in template version of *std::move* and *std::forward*.

std::forward is the easiest to understand (simplified version):

```
template<class T> T&& forward(T&& arguments)
{ // forward an lvalue as either an lvalue or an rvalue
    return (static_cast<T&&>(arguments));
}
```

Which is very similar to the function *f_perfectForwarding*. *T&&* gives a lvale or rvalue depending of the input.

Now we turn our attention to *std::move* (simplified version):

```
template<class T> typename remove_reference<T>::type&&
move(T&& arguments)
{
    return
        static_cast<typename remove_reference<T>::type&&>
        ( arguments );
}
```

**remove_reference<T> &&** remove the reference (**&** or **&&**) and add the rvalue type (**&&**), i.e. cast to a rvalue and return it. With it we can understand how to cast to *T&&* using template.

Last we have to understand the implementation of *remove_reference*, which is a very typical example of template programming. We declare a *struct* with a *typedef* and we specialized it.

```
// generic case
template<typename T> struct remove_reference
{ typedef T type; };

// specialization T&
template<typename T> struct remove_reference<T&>
{ typedef T type; };

// specialization T&&
template<typename T> struct remove_reference<T&&>
{ typedef T type; };
```

# 19. Vector and map 'emplace'

When you 'push_back' an object to a vector, you need first to create it, then copy it, and then destruct the temporary object. With emplace you will create the object "in place" directly:

```cpp
void print(const std::string& str_)
{
    std::cout << str_ << std::endl;
}

struct C11
{
    C11(int a_) { print("constructor"); }
    C11(const C11& c11_) { print("copy constructor"); }
    ~C11() { print("destructor"); }
};

int main()
{
    std::vector<C11> vec1;
    print("___ vec1. push_back _____");
    vec1.push_back(1);

    print("___ vec2. emplace_back _____");
    std::vector<C11> vec2;
    vec2.emplace_back(1);

    print("___ exit _____");
    return 0;
}
```

And the output is:

```
___ vec1. push_back _____
Constructor      // create temporary variable C(1)
move constructor // move temporary variable into the vector
destructor       // remove temporary variable

___ vec2. emplace_back _____
Constructor      // create object in the correct place

___ exit _____
destructor
destructor
```

*(handwritten: Copy?)*

*(handwritten: NB RESERVE or everything is copied anyway!)*

# 20. std::array

An array on the stack with a STL container interface. It is a faster alternative to *std::vector* (which contains an array on the heap) but you need to know its size at compile time.

```cpp
#include <iostream>
#include <array>

int main()
{
    // creation
    std::array<int, 4> arr = { 1,2,3,4 };

    // size
    size_t size = arr.size();

    // display all values
    for (auto i_ : arr)
        std::cout << i_ << " - ";
    std::cout << std::endl;

    // get raw pointer to the array
    int* arr_ptr = arr.data();

    // get STL iterator interface
    auto iter_begin = arr.begin();

    return 0;
}
```

Output:

```
1 - 2 - 3 - 4 -
```

# 21. Hash container

Hash tables in the standard library are implemented as vector of lists. The procedure followed by the container when we insert a value with a key is

- transform the key in an index with a hash function
- get the list on the vector[index] and add an element to it

You can either use the default hash function or define your own.

Similarly, to std::map and std::set, hash tables come in two flavours to accept or not two elements with the same key. To avoid clashes with current external implementations, the name chosen is 'unordered':

- `std::unordered_map`
- `std::unordered_multimap`
- `std::unordered_set`
- `std::unordered_multiset`

## A.  Using default hash functions

For string, the default hash function is quite good. At least if your strings keys have not a special distribution. The interface of *std::unordered_map* is very similar to *std::map*.

```cpp
#include <iostream>
#include <string>
#include <unordered_map>

int main()
{
    std::unordered_map<std::string, int>
        table = { {"ab", 3} , {"pq", 1} , {"os", 3} , {"vo", 2} };

    // add element
    table["mi"] = 32;

    // print all
    for (auto pair : table)
        std::cout << pair.first << ": " << pair.second << std::endl;

    // get ref
    int& ref_mi = table["mi"];

    // find
    auto iter_pair = table.find("ab");
    if(iter_pair != table.end())
    {
        std::cout << "found " << iter_pair->first
              << ": " << iter_pair->second << std::endl;
```

```
        }
        return 0;
    }
```
And the output is:
```
    vo: 2       // for (auto pair : table)
    pq: 1
    ab: 3
    os: 3
    mi: 32
    found ab: 3    // table.find("ab")
```

# B.  Define your own hash function

We can also define our own hash function. In the example below we use our own key and function.

- The hash function must define the 'operator ()(key)', and return a size_t, the index of the list in the vector.
- The key must define the 'operator ==' to be able to differentiate the keys if the index returned by the hash function is already occupied, i.e. the list is not empty.

To define the function we can use the *std::hash<>* for each argument of the key and combine them using the bit shifting and XOR operator.

```cpp
#include <iostream>
#include <string>
#include <unordered_map>

struct Key
{
    int m_a;
    int m_b;
    bool operator ==(const Key& key_) const
    {
        return m_a == key_.m_a && m_b == key_.m_b;
    }
    size_t hashFc() const
    {
        return (std::hash<int>()(m_a) >> 1) ^ (std::hash<int>()(m_b) << 1);
    }
};

struct HashFunction
{
    size_t operator()(const Key& key_) const
    {
```

21. Hash container                                                                                    37

```
        return key_.hashFc();
    }
};


int main()
{
    std::unordered_map<Key, int, HashFunction>
        table = { { {3,2}, 3} , { { 1,2 }, 1} , { { 9,2}, 3} , { { 4,5 }, 2} };

    // print all
    for (auto pair : table)
        std::cout << "(" << pair.first.m_a << "," << pair.first.m_b << "): "
            << pair.second << std::endl;

    return 0;
}
```

And the output is

```
(3,2): 3
(1,2): 1
(4,5): 2
(9,2): 3
```

# 22. std:tuple

## A. Example

Generalization of *std::pair*. From Boost.

```cpp
#include <string>
#include <tuple>

std::tuple<int, double, std::string> triplet(1, 1.1, "1.1");
int i1 = std::get<0>(triplet);
```

## B. Unpack tuple result with std::tie

Python style (more precisely functional language style) using *std::tie*.

```cpp
std::tuple<int, double, std::string> function()
{
    return std::make_tuple(1, 2.3, "2.3");
}

int main()
{
    int integer;
    std::string string;

    // using std::ignore if you want to ...ignore one of the element
    std::tie(integer, std::ignore, string) = function();

    std::cout << "integer = " << integer << std::endl;
    std::cout << "string = " << string << std::endl;

    return 0;
}
```

And the output:

```
integer = 1
string = 2.3
```

# 23. External template

Used to avoid the instantiation of the template in a cpp file and therefore avoid multiple compilations of the same code.

For example, we have a full defined template in a Header file *Header.h*:

```cpp
#include <vector>
#include <algorithm>

template <typename T1>
struct BigTemplate
{
    T1 m_a;
    std::vector<T1> m_vector;
    BigTemplate(const T1& a_) : m_a(a_) {}
    const T1& get() { return m_a; }
    void sort()
    {
        std::sort(m_vector.begin(), m_vector.end());
    }
};
```

Then we use it in our cpp file *SourceMain.cpp*

```cpp
#include <string>
#include "Header.h"

// no instantation of template for this file
extern template struct BigTemplate<int>;
extern template struct BigTemplate<double>;
extern template struct BigTemplate<std::string>;

int main()
{
    BigTemplate<int> big_int(3);
    std::cout << big_int.get() << std::endl;

    BigTemplate<double> big_double(5);
    std::cout << big_double.get() << std::endl;

    BigTemplate<std::string> big_string("'3'");
    std::cout << big_string.get() << std::endl;

    return 0;
}
```

The *extern* keyword tells the compiler to not instantiate the template in the compiled object file. We have therefore to instantiate it in another file, here *Source.cpp*:

```cpp
#include "Header.h"
#include <string>

// force instantation
template BigTemplate<int>;
template BigTemplate<double>;
template BigTemplate<std::string>;
```

# 24. nullptr

Use **nullptr** keyword instead of 0 to initialize a raw pointer. In some case it will help for overloading function with int or void* signature. In any case it is considered as *good practice* to use nullptr.

```cpp
int* ptr = nullptr;
```

If you have some overloading functions with a signature of pointer, you will have a compilation error without defining also the one for nullptr_t type:

```cpp
void function(int* ptr_) {}
void function(double* ptr_) {}
//void function(nullptr_t ptr_) {}

int main()
{
    function(nullptr);

    return 0;
}
```

And the result of the compilation:

```
error C2668: 'function': ambiguous call to overloaded function
note: could be 'void function(double *)'
note: or        'void function(int *)'
```

We need to define the function with the type *nullptr_t*:

```cpp
void function(nullptr_t ptr_) {}
```

Also if you want to call a template without giving explicitly the argument type, 0 will always be an int, not a null pointer:

```cpp
#include <iostream>

void f(int*) { std::cout << "int ptr" << std::endl; }
void f(double) { std::cout << "double" << std::endl; }

template <typename T> void f_t(const T& t_) { f(t_); }

int main()
{
    // double
    f_t(0);

    // int ptr
    f_t(nullptr);
```

```
    return 0;
}
```

# 25. lambda

lambda is a way to create function without too much hassle. It is very convenient but be careful because you can have dangling reference (see item 25.F)

## A. lambda in another function

Imagine that you want to create a function to multiply a double by 2:

```cpp
double notLambda(const double& a_)
{
    return 2. * a_;
}
```

With lambda you can create the function inline in the code:

```cpp
auto lambda = [](const double& a_) { return 2. * a_; };
double res = lambda(3.); // res = 2*3 = 6
```

## B. lambda using an external variable

in C03 we use a class functor when we want to use an external variable:

```cpp
struct lambda
{
    double m_c;
    lambda(const double& c_) : m_c(c_) {}
    double operator()(const double& a_) const
    {
        return m_c * a_;
    }
};

int main()
{
    double c = 2;
    double res = lambda(c)(3); // res = 2*3 = 6

    return 0;
}
```

With lambda we can use a much more concise form

```cpp
int main()
{
    double c = 2;
    auto lambda = [=](const double& a_) { return c * a_; };
    double res = lambda(3); // res = 2*3 = 6
```

```
        return 0;
}
```

The '=' sign means that we copy the variable **c** before using it in the lambda. You can also use it by reference:

```
auto lambda = [&](const double& a_) { return c * a_; };
```

We can also specify the name of the variable (to avoid referencing an unwanted variables):

```
auto lambda1 = [&c](const double& a_) { return c * a_; };
auto lambda2 = [ c](const double& a_) { return c * a_; };
```

## C.  Specify the return type

The return type is optional and will be deduced by the compiler. You can, however, define it using '->':

```
auto lambda = [&c](const double& a_)->double { return c * a_; };
```

## D.  Using lambda in std::algorithm

Lamda functions are particularly powerful in combination with algorithms. For example in the program below we add a value to each element of a vector:

```
#include <vector>
#include <algorithm>

int main()
{
    int c = 4;
    auto lambda = [&](int& a_) { a_ += c; };

    std::vector<int> vec1 = { 1,2,3,4 };
    std::for_each(vec1.begin(), vec1.end(), lambda);
    // vec1 = { 5,6,7,8 }

    return 0;
}
```
Personally I would prefer a loop, but it seems that the complicated and un-debuggable way is trendy…

## E.  lambda in functionsignature

We can pass std::function<fc_signature>. See item .26 for an example.

25. lambda

## F. lambda with dangling reference

We must be very careful when using lambda and passing it around. In the example below we refer a reference (*i_*) which does not exist anymore

```cpp
// function returning a lambda
template <typename T>
auto f1(T i_)
{
    // return a lambda with a dangling reference
    // since i_ will go out of scope at the return of the function
    auto lambda = [&] {return  i_ + 3; };
    return lambda;
}

int main()
{
    // lambda: no dangling reference
    // i exists
    int i = 2;
    auto lambda = [&] {return  i + 3; };
    int a_ok = lambda(); // 2+3=5

    // create a lambda with a dangling reference
    auto lamda_missingRef = f1(2);
    // example of result:
    // 14621279 instead of 2+3=5
    // i_ is out of scope
    int a_missingRef = lamda_missingRef();

    return 0;
}
```

# 26. std::function<...>

Useful to store function, instead of a pointer of function, for example when integrating a function, .... You can also use *auto* . From boost::function.

```cpp
#include <string>
#include <functional>
#include <iostream>

int f1(int i_) { return i_; }

struct C11
{
    int m_i;
    int f1(const int& i_) { return i_ + m_i; }
};

int main()
{
    // function
    std::function<int(int)> g1 = f1;
    auto g1_auto = f1;
    std::cout << g1(3) << std::endl;
    std::cout << g1_auto(3) << std::endl;

    // member function
    C11 c11;
    c11.m_i = 2;
    std::function<int(int)> g2 = std::bind(&C11::f1, &c11, std::placeholders::_1);
    auto g2_auto = std::bind(&C11::f1, &c11, std::placeholders::_1);
    std::cout << g2(3) << std::endl;
    std::cout << g2_auto(3) << std::endl;

    return 0;
}
```

And the output is:

```
3
3
5
5
```

# 27. Smart pointers: std::shared_ptr

From Boost. Reference counted. You can copy it. You must add *#include <memory>* before using it.

## A.  std::make_shared

You can create you shared pointer directly (method 1 in the program below) or using the function *std::make_shared* (method 2). The second method is better for exception handling and slightly faster to write. However, it can't handle custom delete and if you need intellisense in Visual Studio you need to use the first method

```cpp
#include <memory>

// method 1:
std::shared_ptr<int> sharedPtr1(new int(12));

// method 2:
std::shared_ptr<int> sharedPtr2(std::make_shared<int>(12));
```

## B.  Using custom deleter

You can use your own custom delete. Very useful if you have only a raw pointer from an old interface and need to send a shared_ptr to your "new" library. In this case the deleter will not delete anything. In the following example we use a lambda but we can also use a free function.

```cpp
#include <memory>
auto deleter = [](int* pi) { delete pi; };
std::shared_ptr<int> sharedPtr(new int(12), deleter);
```

# 28. Smart pointers: std:unique_ptr

The sequel of the infamous auto_ptr. The memory can't be shared. The unique_ptr owns the memory, and will free it when the pointer goes out of scope.

## A.   Move

If you need to create a vector of unique pointer, or a shared_ptr from a unique_ptr you must use std::move.

```cpp
#include <memory>
#include <vector>

std::unique_ptr<int> uniquePtr(new int(12));
std::shared_ptr<int> sharedPtr(std::move(uniquePtr));
// uniquePtr = 0

std::unique_ptr<int> uniquePtr2(new int(13));
std::vector<std::unique_ptr<int>> vec;
vec.push_back(std::move(uniquePtr2));
// uniquePtr2 = 0
```

## B.   Using custom deleter

Contrary to the shared_ptr you need to specify the type of the deleter. We use decltype() explained in item 7:

```cpp
#include <memory>
auto deleter = [](int* pi) { delete pi; };
std::unique_ptr<int, decltype(deleter)> uniquePtr(new int(12), deleter);
```

## C.   Pimpl

Unique_ptr is perfect for a *pointer implementation* pimpl: no need to delete the pointer explicitly and no need of a shared_ptr here.

In the file *Header.h*:

```cpp
#include <memory>

class Pimpl; // forward declaration

class MyClass
{
    std::unique_ptr<Pimpl> m_pimpl;
public:
    MyClass();
};
```

In file *Source.cpp*:

```cpp
#include "Header.h"

class Pimpl {};

MyClass::MyClass() : m_pimpl(std::make_unique<Pimpl>()) {}
```

# 29. Smart pointers: std::weak_ptr

Possibility to query at demand the shared_ptr without holding a reference, and therefore without increasing the count

```cpp
#include <iostream>
#include <string>
#include <memory>

void print(const std::string& str_)
{
    std::cout << str_ << std::endl;
}

int main()
{
    std::weak_ptr<int> weakPtr;
    {
        std::shared_ptr<int> sharedPtr(new int(12));
        weakPtr = sharedPtr;

        std::shared_ptr<int> getSharedPtr1 = weakPtr.lock();
        print(getSharedPtr1 ? "getSharedPtr1: got it"
                            : "getSharedPtr1 Empty");
    } // sharedPtr removed

    // weak.lock will give an empty shared_ptr
    std::shared_ptr<int> getSharedPtr2 = weakPtr.lock();
    print(getSharedPtr2 ? "getSharedPtr2: got it"
                        : "getSharedPtr2: Empty");

    return 0;
}
```

And the output is:

```
getSharedPtr1: got it
getSharedPtr2: Empty
```

# 30. Enum

Strongly typed enumeration. Advantage

- No namespace pollution
- No enum to integer conversion by default
- Possibility of forward declaration
- Type value can be any sign or un-sign integer

As seen in the program below, the new enum is better typed.

```cpp
enum C03 { C03red, C03blue };
enum class C11 { red, blue };
enum class C12 { red, blue };   // OK: no name pollution

int main()
{
    // no name pollution in C11
    C03 c03red = C03red; // name pollution
    C11 c11red = C11::red;

    // conversion to int
    int c03redInt = C03red;
    int c11redInt = static_cast<int>(C11::red);

    // conversion from int
    C03 c03blue = static_cast<C03>(1); // blue
    C11 c11blue = static_cast<C11>(1); // blue

    // could give an error or we could have a dynamic_cast!
    C03 c03noColor = static_cast<C03>(4); // no error
    C11 c11noColor = static_cast<C11>(4); // no error!

    return 0;
}
```

If you want to specify the type of your enum (default is integer) you can include the header *cstdint and use any sign or un-sign integer*:

```cpp
#include <cstdint>
enum class C11: std::int64_t { red, blue };
```

# 31. long long

C++ 11 introduced *long long* type with at least a 64 bits storage.

For double we still have the long double with gcc but this does not help with Visual,

```cpp
std::cout << "on windows x64, VS 2015" << std::endl;
std::cout << "sizeof(int) = " << sizeof(int) << std::endl;
std::cout << "sizeof(long int) = " << sizeof(long int) << std::endl;
std::cout << "sizeof(long long int) = " << sizeof(long long int) << std::endl;
std::cout << "sizeof(unsigned long long int) = " << sizeof(unsigned long long int) << std::endl;
std::cout << "sizeof(double) = " << sizeof(double) << std::endl;
std::cout << "sizeof(long double) = " << sizeof(long double) << std::endl;

int int1 = 8446744073709550592;
long int long_int = 8446744073709550592;
long long int long_long = 8446744073709550592ll;
unsigned long long int unsign_long_long = 18446744073709550592ull;
double pi_double = 3.14159265358979323846264338327950288419716939937510;
long double pi_long_double =
        3.14159265358979323846264338327950288419716939937510L;

std::cout.precision(50);
std::cout << std::endl;
std::cout << "int             = " << "8446744073709550592" << std::endl;
std::cout << "int1            = " << int1 << std::endl;
std::cout << "long_int        = " << long_int << std::endl;
std::cout << "long_long       = " << long_long << std::endl;
std::cout << "unsign_long_long = " << unsign_long_long << std::endl;
std::cout << "pi_double       = " << pi_double << std::endl;
std::cout << "pi_long_double  = " << pi_long_double << std::endl;
std::cout << "pi              = " << "3.14159265358979323846264338327950288419716939937510" << std::endl;
```

And the output is:

```
on windows x64, VS 2015
sizeof(int) = 4
sizeof(long int) = 4
sizeof(long long int) = 8
sizeof(unsigned long long int) = 8
sizeof(double) = 8
sizeof(long double) = 8

int              = 8446744073709550592
int1             = 1981283328
long_int         = 1981283328
long_long        = 8446744073709550592
unsign_long_long = 18446744073709550592
```

```
pi_double       = 3.1415926535897931159979634685441851615905 76171875
pi_long_double  = 3.1415926535897931159979634685441851615905 76171875
pi              = 3.14159265358979323846264338327950288419716939937510
```

# 32. cstdint: sized integer

What is the size of an *int*? It depends of the platform. It can be a 32-bit or a 64-bit, or even a 128-bit. This lack of standard can bring numerical problems that are hard to resolve like between 32-bit windows and 64-bit linux results. Previously in <stdint>. C++ 11 moves it in std.:

- int8_t, int16_t, int32_t, int64_t
- uInt8_t, uint16_t, uint32_t, uint64_t

```cpp
#include <iostream>
#include <cstdint>

int main()
{
    std::cout << "on windows x64, VS 2015" << std::endl;
    std::cout << "sizeof(int8_t  ) = " << sizeof(int8_t) << std::endl;
    std::cout << "sizeof(int16_t ) = " << sizeof(int16_t) << std::endl;
    std::cout << "sizeof(int32_t ) = " << sizeof(int32_t) << std::endl;
    std::cout << "sizeof(int64_t ) = " << sizeof(int64_t) << std::endl;
    std::cout << "sizeof(uint8_t ) = " << sizeof(uint8_t) << std::endl;
    std::cout << "sizeof(uint16_t) = " << sizeof(uint16_t) << std::endl;
    std::cout << "sizeof(uint32_t) = " << sizeof(uint32_t) << std::endl;
    std::cout << "sizeof(uint64_t) = " << sizeof(uint64_t) << std::endl;

    return 0;
}
```

And the output on windows x64, VS 2015 (results in bits = 8-bit)

```
on windows x64, VS 2015
sizeof(int8_t  ) = 1
sizeof(int16_t ) = 2
sizeof(int32_t ) = 4
sizeof(int64_t ) = 8
sizeof(uint8_t ) = 1
sizeof(uint16_t) = 2
sizeof(uint32_t) = 4
sizeof(uint64_t) = 8
```

In MSVS, these type have been implemented using *typedef*:

```cpp
typedef signed char        int8_t;
typedef short              int16_t;
typedef int                int32_t;
typedef long long          int64_t;
typedef unsigned char      uint8_t;
typedef unsigned short     uint16_t;
typedef unsigned int       uint32_t;
typedef unsigned long long uint64_t;
```

You can implement a random number generator using these types, if you do not want to use the standard library tool explained in item 37.

# 33. static_assert

Assert at compile time similarly to BOOST_STATIC_ASSERT

```cpp
#include <type_traits>

struct C11
{
    int m_a;
    int m_b;
};

int main()
{
    static_assert(sizeof(C11) == sizeof(int),"C11 has some new arguments");
    return 0;
}
```

And the output of the compilation on Visual Studio is:

```
error C2338: C11 has some new arguments
```

# 34. Variadic template

Template functions with any number of arguments. The principle is to create another overloading function with only a definite number of parameters and using a recursive procedure. For example, we create a convert to string function:

```cpp
#include <string>
#include <sstream>

template <typename T>
void c2s_help(std::ostringstream& o, const T& x)
{
    o << x;
}

template <typename T, typename... Args>
void c2s_help(std::ostringstream& o, const T& x, Args... args)
{
    c2s_help(o, x); // add first element
    c2s_help(o, args...); // call recursive
}


template <typename... Args>
std::string c2s(Args... args)
{
    std::ostringstream o;
    c2s_help(o, args...);
    return o.str();
}

int main()
{
    // str = "I am 25"
    std::string str = c2s("I ", "am ", 25);

    return 0;
}
```

# 35. Exceptions

## A.  std::exception

*std::exception_ptr* and *std::current_exception()* were introduced in C++ 11. *exception_ptr* can hold an exception and can be passed around, even to another thread. *current_exception()* is a convenient way to get the current exception after a catch with (...):

```cpp
std::exception_ptr exceptionPtr;
try
{
    throw std::runtime_error("error!");
}
catch (...)
{
    exceptionPtr = std::current_exception();
    // possible:
    // std::rethrow_exception(exceptionPtr);
}
```

## B.  noexcept

*noexcept*, for "no exception", replaces *throw()* to let the compiler (and your clients) knows that no exception will go out of the function. If an exception is emitted by the function, the program will crash. Knowing that the function does not emit exception allows your compiler (and your clients) to optimize the code. However, be careful when introducing *noexcept*. Your function could call another function which is not exception free and then you need a try catch in your function to guarantee the *noexcept*.

```cpp
void functionThrow()
{ throw "rrr"; }

void functionCrash() noexcept
{ functionThrow(); }

void functionNoCrash() noexcept
{
    try { functionThrow(); }
    catch (...) {}
}

int main()
{
    // this function will not crash the program
    functionNoCrash();
```

```cpp
        // this function will    crash the program
        // even with the try catch
        try { functionCrash(); }
        catch (...) {}

        return 0;
    }
```

We can write also

```cpp
    noexcept(true) // no exception
    noexcept(false) // may throw exception
```

## C. noexcept operator

*noexcept* can also be used as an operator. For example, in our program we could write

```cpp
    // this function will not crash the program
    void functionCrash() noexcept(noexcept(functionThrow()))
    {
        functionThrow();
    }
```

The operator **noexcept(functionThrow())** will return *false* at **compile time** because the function *functionThrow()* is not marked as *noexcept*. Therefore, the resulting signature will be

```cpp
    // this function will not crash the program
    void functionCrash() noexcept(false)
    {
        functionThrow();
    }
```

And calling this function will not crash the program

# 36. Time utilities

Several classes are now presents in std.

- *std::chrono::system_clock* is the C time system. If the user changes the time, the future time can be less than the current time.
- *std::chrono::steady_clock* guarantees that the time obtained never decreases.
- *std::chrono::high_resolution_clock* is a "high resolution" time but is compiler dependent

In the example below we use *std::steady_clock*...

```cpp
#include <iostream>
#include <chrono>
#include <thread>

int main()
{
    // start as std::chrono::steady_clock::time_point
    auto start = std::chrono::steady_clock::now();
    std::this_thread::sleep_for (std::chrono::milliseconds (2534));
    auto duration = std::chrono::steady_clock::now() - start;

    // duration_... as long long
    auto duration_s =
std::chrono::duration_cast<std::chrono::seconds>(duration).count();
    auto duration_ms =
std::chrono::duration_cast<std::chrono::milliseconds>(duration).count();
    auto duration_micros =
std::chrono::duration_cast<std::chrono::microseconds>(duration).count();

    std::cout << "duration = " << duration_s << " s" << std::endl;
    std::cout << "duration = " << duration_ms << " ms" << std::endl;
    std::cout << "duration = " << duration_micros << " micro s" <<
std::endl;
    return 0;
}
```

And the output is:

```
duration = 2 s
duration = 2534 ms
duration = 2534296 micro s
```

More examples in the thread section.

# 37. Random generator

A long awaited portable random generator in STL   **Error! Bookmark not defined.**

```cpp
#include <iostream>

#include <random>
#include <functional> // for std::bind

int main()
{
    std::default_random_engine engine;

    // dice
    std::uniform_int_distribution<int> ran_int_1_6(1, 6);
    std::cout << "ran_int_1_6 : " << ran_int_1_6(engine) << std::endl;
    std::cout << "ran_int_1_6 : " << ran_int_1_6(engine) << std::endl;

    // using bind
    auto dice = std::bind(ran_int_1_6, engine);
    std::cout << "dice        : " << dice() << std::endl;
    std::cout << "dice        : " << dice() << std::endl;

    // normal(nu, sigma)
    std::normal_distribution<> ran_normal(0, 0.2);
    auto normal = std::bind(ran_normal, engine);
    std::cout << "normal      : " << normal() << std::endl;
    std::cout << "normal      : " << normal() << std::endl;

    return 0;
}
```

And the output is:

```
ran_int_1_6 : 3
ran_int_1_6 : 1
dice        : 3
dice        : 6
normal      : -0.205807
normal      : -0.141525
```

# 38. Regular expressions

Mainly boost::regex. See examples in the following program:

```cpp
#include <iostream>
#include <regex>

int main()
{
    std::string s = R"(A sentence to use as example )" "\n"
        R"(... to study std:: regular expressions)" ;
    std::cout << s << std::endl << std::endl;

    // look for the number of words
    {
        std::string lookFor = "(\\S+)";
        std::regex lookForRegex(lookFor);
        auto begin = std::sregex_iterator(s.begin(), s.end(), lookForRegex);
        auto end = std::sregex_iterator();
        std::cout << "number of words: "
            << std::distance(begin, end) << std::endl;
    }

    // look for an element
    {
        std::string lookFor = "example";
        std::regex lookForRegex(lookFor);
        bool found = std::regex_search(s, lookForRegex);
        std::cout << (found ? "" : "Not ")
            << "found in text: " << lookFor << std::endl;
    }

    // look for an element, ignore case
    {
        std::string lookFor = "EXAMPLE";
        std::regex lookForRegex(lookFor, std::regex_constants::icase);
        bool found = std::regex_search(s, lookForRegex);
        std::cout << (found ? "" : "Not ")
            << "found in text (ignore case): " << lookFor << std::endl;
    }

    // look for all words beginning by "ex"
    {
        std::string  lookFor = "\\b(ex)([^ ]*)";
        std::string str(s);
        std::smatch match;
        std::regex lookForRegex(lookFor);   // matches words beginning by "sub"
```

```
        std::cout << "look for all words beginning by 'ex'" <<
std::endl;
        while (std::regex_search(str, match, lookForRegex))
        {
            std::cout<< "found: " << " " << match[0] << std::endl;
            str = match.suffix().str();
        }
    }

    return 0;
}
```

And the output is:

```
A sentence to use as example
... to study std:: regular expressions

number of words: 12
found in text: example
found in text (ignore case): EXAMPLE
look for all words beginning by 'ex'
found:   example
found:   expressions
```

Links:

- http://www.regular-expressions.info/
- https://support.google.com/a/answer/1371417?hl=en

# 39. User-defined literals

You can define your own literal for example:

```cpp
constexpr long double operator"" _km(long double d_)
{
    return 1000.*d_;
}

int main()
{
    // d = 1000
    double d = 1._km;

    return 0;
}
```

You must use **operator""** and the literal you want (here **_km**). Note the input of

**operator"" _km(long double d_)**

can't be a reference and can't a double, it must one of the following type:

```
unsigned long long int
long double
char
wchar_t
char16_t
char32_t
const char*, std::size_t
const wchar_t*, std::size_t
const char16_t*, std::size_t
const char32_t*, std::size_t
const char*
```

# 40. constexpr

Not available in VS 2013.

*constexpr*, constant expression, will let the compiler determines at compile time the constant value, if possible. If the value is indeed accessible at compile time, this expression can be used as a constant, for example to specify the size of an array.

A value can be constexpr but also a function. In this case, if possible, the value will be calculated at compile time, not run time. Be careful, however, to not let you carry over too far. Mainly it is meta-programming, i.e. you can't debug it. Moreover, in C++ 11, the function must be a single executable statement, i.e. a return. In C++ 14 this is more relaxed but it is not implemented with VS 2015 compiler.

```cpp
constexpr int factorial(int n_)
{
    return (n_ > 1) ? n_*factorial(n_-1) : 1;
}

int main()
{
    std::array<int, factorial(4)> array;

    return 0;
}
```

# 41. Union

Not available in VS 2013.

The union in C++ 11 are more powerful than standard C union. Mainly they can have a constructor, destructor, copy, move, and assignment constructors & operators. Moreover, it can accept member variables with constructors like string or vector. However you will need to call the constructor and destructor for these variables explicitly:

```cpp
#include <string>

using namespace std;
union U
{
    int m_i;
    std::string m_s;

    U() {}
    ~U() {}
};

int main()
{
    U u;

    // set as integer
    u.m_i = 3;

    // set as string : need to call the placement new
    new (&u.m_s) std::string("toto");

    // set as integer
    // need to manually call the destructor for the string
    u.m_s.~string();
    u.m_i = 2;

    return 0;
}
```

You can enter this method for the string inside the union, defining the assignment operator = ... and create ... your own variant.

# 42. Attribute

Not available in VS2013.

Similar to #pragma. Compiler dependent.

```
[[noreturn]]   void f1() { } // VS2015: recognized attribute
[[deprecated]] void f2() { } // VS2015: recognized attribute for C++ 14
[[toto]]       void f3() { } // VS2015: warning C5030: attribute 'toto' is
not recognized
```

# 43. std::algorithm

C11 introduced several new algorithms. The main focus is to "increase the level of abstraction and provide more opportunities for the compiler to optimize the code like parallelisation and/or vectorization". My summary is that the objective is to avoid loops. A selection of useful algorithms are presented in this item. All algorithms are accessible here:
http://en.cppreference.com/w/cpp/algorithm

## A. minmax_element

Return a pair with the minimum and maximum of a range. If you need only the minimum or maximum you can use *std::min()* and *std::max()*.

```cpp
#include <iostream>
#include <vector>
#include <algorithm>

int main()
{
    std::vector<int> vec = {1,40,20,-3,10,15,-3};

    // pair
    auto minMaxPair = std::minmax_element (vec.begin(), vec.end());

    std::cout << "minimum = " << *minMaxPair.first << std::endl;
    std::cout << "maximum = " << *minMaxPair.second << std::endl;

    return 0;
}
```

## B. std::all_of, std::any_of, std::none_of

- std::all_of(...): return true if all elements in the range satisfy a condition
- std::any_of(...): return true if any element in the range satisfies a condition
- std::none_of(...): return true if no elements in the range satisfies a condition

```cpp
#include <vector>
#include <algorithm>

int main()
{
    std::vector<int> vec = {1,40,20,-3,10,15,-3};

    auto lambdaPositive = [](int i_) { return i_ >= 0; };

    // allPositive = false
```

```cpp
    bool allPositive = std::all_of(vec.begin(), vec.end(),
lambdaPositive);

    // anyPositive = true
    bool anyPositive = std::any_of(vec.begin(), vec.end(),
lambdaPositive);

    // nonePositive = false
    bool nonePositive = std::none_of(vec.begin(), vec.end(),
lambdaPositive);

    return 0;
}
```

## C.  std::is_sorted

Return true if the range is sorted. We can specify the condition. The default condition is *greater than*:

```cpp
#include <vector>
#include <algorithm>

int main()
{
    std::vector<int> vec = {1,3,6,8,9,10};

    // isSorted More = true
    bool isSorted = std::is_sorted(vec.begin(), vec.end());

    // isSorted Less = false
    auto sortLess = [](int i_, int j_) { return i_ > j_; };
    bool isSortedLess = std::is_sorted(vec.begin(), vec.end(), sortLess);


    return 0;
}
```

## D.  std::count, count_if

Return the number of elements in a range satisfying a condition:

```cpp
#include <vector>
#include <algorithm>

int main()
{
    std::vector<int> vec = {1,6,10,1,-5,7};

    // count nb of elt == value => count(1) = 2
    size_t count_equal = std::count(vec.begin(), vec.end(),1);
```

```cpp
    // count nb of values > 3 => count_if(val>3) = 3
    auto conditionGreater = [](int i_) { return i_ > 3; };
    size_t count_greater = std::count_if(vec.begin(), vec.end(), conditionGreater);

    return 0;
}
```

# E. std::find, find_if

Find the first element in a range satisfying a condition:

```cpp
#include <vector>
#include <algorithm>

int main()
{
    std::vector<int> vec = {1,6,10,1,-5,7};

    // get iterator first element == value => find(1) = iterator_0
    auto find_equal = std::find(vec.begin(), vec.end(),1);
    size_t index_equal = std::distance(vec.begin(), find_equal);

    // get iterator first element == condition => find_i(val>3) = iterator_1
    auto conditionGreater = [](int i_) { return i_ > 3; };
    auto find_greater = std::find_if(vec.begin(), vec.end(), conditionGreater);
    size_t index_greater = std::distance(vec.begin(), find_greater);

    return 0;
}
```

# F. std::copy_if

Copy a range to another range for values satisfying a condition:

```cpp
#include <vector>
#include <algorithm>

int main()
{
    std::vector<int> vec = {1,6,10,1,-5,7};

    // create a vector with elements > 3

    // the condition
    auto conditionGreater = [](int i_) { return i_ > 3; };

    // create vector result same size as original
```

43. std::algorithm

```cpp
    // vec_copy_greater = {0,0,0,0,0,0}
    std::vector<int> vec_copy_greater(vec.size());

    // put all elements with the condition in the new vector
    // return iterator after the last copy
    // vec_copy_greater = {6,10,7,0,0,0}
    auto iterEnd = std::copy_if(vec.begin(), vec.end(),
                    vec_copy_greater.begin(), conditionGreater);

    // resize the vector
    // vec_copy_greater = {6,10,7}
    // size = 3
    size_t size = std::distance(vec_copy_greater.begin(), iterEnd);
    vec_copy_greater.resize(size);

    return 0;
}
```

# G. std::iota, std::generate

- std::iota. Fill a range by increasing values, starting from an initial value. Need `#include <numeric>`.
- std::generate. Fill a range by a result from a function

```cpp
#include <vector>
#include <algorithm>
#include <numeric>

int main()
{
    // std::iota: {ini, ini+1, ini+2, ...}
    // need #include <numeric>
    // vec1 = {2,3,4,5}
    std::vector<int> vec1(4);
    std::iota(vec1.begin(), vec1.end(), 2);

    // std::generate: {function(), function(), function(), ...}
    // vec1 = {2,4,6,8}
    std::vector<int> vec2(4);
    int n = 2;
    std::generate(vec2.begin(), vec2.end(), [&n] { n += 2;  return n; });

    return 0;
}
```

# H.  std::transform

Transform a range to another (or the same) range, applying a function. In the example below we add 2 to each element of the vector.

```cpp
#include <vector>
#include <algorithm>

int main()
{
    // std::transform: {function(vec[0]), function(vec[1]), ...}
    std::vector<int> vec = {2,4,5,8};
    std::transform(vec.begin(), vec.end(), vec.begin()
                    , [](int val) { return val+2; });
    // vec = { 4,6,7,10 };

    return 0;
}
```

# 44. std::bind

*std::bind* is used to bind the arguments of a function, or a lambda, with values without calling the function. This creates a function object which can be called. We can use *std::placeholders* to provide only some variables of the original function. In this case, the other variables must be provided when calling the new function. See example below.

```cpp
#include <functional>

int main()
{
    // create a function binding the lambda to a value
    auto lambda0 = [](int i0_) { return 2*i0_; };
    auto function0 = std::bind(lambda0, 2);
    int res0 = function0(); // res0 = 4

    // create a function binding the lambda to a value
    // and a placeholder _1: first element in 'function1'
    // need:    using namespace std::placeholders;
    using namespace std::placeholders;
    auto lambda1 = [](int i0_, int i1_) { return 2*i0_ + i1_; };
    auto function1 = std::bind(lambda1, 2, _1);
    int res1 = function1(4); // res1 = 2*2+4 = 8

    // create a function binding the lambda to a value
    // and 2 placeholders _1 and _2: first and second elements in 'function2'
    using namespace std::placeholders;
    auto lambda3 = [](int i0_, int i1_) { return 2*i0_+i1_; };
    // be careful of the order of _1 and _2
    // function3(x, y) = lambda3(y, x)
    auto function3 = std::bind(lambda3, _2, _1);
    int res3 = function3(2,4); // res1 = 2*4+2 = 10

    // using reference
    using namespace std::placeholders;
    auto lambda4 = [](int i0_, int i1_) { return 2 * i0_ + i1_; };
    int i0 = 2;
    auto function4 = std::bind(lambda4, std::ref(i0), _1);
    i0 = 5; // because of std::ref(i0), this value will be used
    int res4 = function4(4); // res1 = 2*5+4 = 14

    // using reference
    using namespace std::placeholders;
    // i0_ change the value in the function
    auto lambda5 = [](int& i0_, int i1_) { ++i0_;  return 2 * i0_ + i1_; };
    i0 = 2;
    auto function5 = std::bind(lambda5, std::ref(i0), _1);
    int res5 = function5(4); // ++i0_ => i0 = 3 => res1 = 2*3+4 = 10
```

```cpp
    // i0 = 3

    // using constant reference
    using namespace std::placeholders;
    auto lambda6 = [](const int& i0_, int i1_) { return 2 * i0_ + i1_; };
    i0 = 2;
    auto function6 = std::bind(lambda6, std::cref(i0), _1);
    int res6 = function6(4); //   res1 = 2*2+4 = 8
    // i0 = 2

    return 0;
}
```

# 45. Concurrency: std::async

Multitasks. Usage of std::async causes the running process to be multithreaded with the management of the threads handled by the STL. Much more robust than managing the threads yourself.

## A.  Example

```cpp
#include <iostream>
#include <future>
#include <chrono>
#include <thread>

// a task to run asynchronously
int f1(int i_)
{
    std::this_thread::sleep_for(std::chrono::seconds(i_));
    return i_;
}

// print the duration
void printDuration(std::chrono::steady_clock::time_point start_)
{
    auto duration = std::chrono::steady_clock::now() - start_;
    auto duration_ms =
std::chrono::duration_cast<std::chrono::milliseconds>(duration).count();
    std::cout << "----------- duration from start = " << duration_ms << " ms" << std::endl;
}

int main()
{
    auto start = std::chrono::steady_clock::now();

    // launch 4 tasks
    auto a0 = std::async(&f1, 1);
    auto a1 = std::async(&f1, 1);
    auto a2 = std::async(&f1, 3);
    auto a3 = std::async(&f1, 2);

    // print result
    printDuration(start);

    // wait until a0 is done
    std::cout << "a0 = " << a0.get() << std::endl;
    printDuration(start);

    // wait until a1 is done
    std::cout << "a1 = " << a1.get() << std::endl;
```

```
        printDuration(start);

        // wait until a2 is done
        std::cout << "a2 = " << a2.get() << std::endl;
        printDuration(start);

        // wait until a3 is done
        std::cout << "a3 = " << a3.get() << std::endl;
        printDuration(start);

        return 0;
    }
```

And the output is:

```
    ----------- duration from start = 0 ms
    a0 = 1
    ----------- duration from start = 1002 ms
    a1 = 1
    ----------- duration from start = 1009 ms
    a2 = 3
    ----------- duration from start = 3002 ms
    a3 = 2
    ----------- duration from start = 3006 ms
```

## B.  Options: deferred

By default the status of the task launch is either *std::launch::async* or *std::launch::deferred*. Deferred means that it will wait until the current thread is free, *async* that the task run asynchronously. In the default case the library/OS will decide what is the "best" way to launch the task. If you want to be sure of the way to launch you need to specify the option.   In the example below we run all tasks on the same thread:

```
    auto a0 = std::async(std::launch::deferred,&f1, 1);
    auto a1 = std::async(std::launch::deferred,&f1, 1);
    auto a2 = std::async(std::launch::deferred,&f1, 3);
    auto a3 = std::async(std::launch::deferred,&f1, 2);
```

and the output could be

```
    ----------- duration from start = 0 ms
    a0 = 1
    ----------- duration from start = 1004 ms
    a1 = 1
    ----------- duration from start = 2011 ms
    a2 = 3
    ----------- duration from start = 5018 ms
    a3 = 2
    ----------- duration from start = 7025 ms
```

To check if the status is deferred/ready/timeout, you can check a condition similar to:

45. Concurrency: std::async

```cpp
bool deferred = a1.wait_for(std::chrono::seconds(0)) ==
std::future_status::deferred;
```

# 46. Concurrency: std::atomic

Mutex are slow. Atomic variables may be faster, but it is not certain. You do not need to lock them manually because all operations (+/-/=) will be an "atomic" operation, i.e. certified to have no race problem between threads for read and write. Note that these operations could be implemented using a lock under the hood. Moreover, you are limited to machine data type (int, long, char) and operation (+/-/=).

```cpp
#include <iostream>
#include <future>
#include <atomic>

std::atomic<int> i1 = 0;

struct C11
{
    std::atomic<int> m_shared;
    void add_One() { ++m_shared; }
    void take_One() { --m_shared; }
    int get() const { return m_shared.load(); }
};

C11 c11;

int add(size_t n_)
{
    for (size_t i = 0; i < n_; ++i)
        c11.add_One();
    return c11.get();
}

int take(size_t n_)
{
    for (size_t i = 0; i < n_; ++i)
        c11.take_One();
    return c11.get();
}

int main()
{
    auto future0 = std::async(std::launch::async, &add , 500000);
    auto future1 = std::async(std::launch::async, &take, 400000);

    future0.get();
    future1.get();

    std::cout << "result = " << c11.get() << std::endl;

    return 0;
}
```

And the output is, as expected, 100,000 = 500,000 – 400,000

```
result = 100000
```

# 47. Concurrency: Mutex

Mutex are used to lock a shared memory to avoid threads clashes when several threads want to access it at the same time.

## A.  Example

In the program below we create several threads to push back some integers in a shared vector.

```cpp
#include <iostream>
#include <vector>
#include <memory>
#include <thread>
#include <mutex>

std::vector<int> vec_shared;
std::mutex mutex;

void pushBack(int nb_)
{
    // lock mutex
    std::lock_guard<std::mutex> lock(mutex);

    // operation on shared vector
    for (int i = 0; i < 100; ++i)
        vec_shared.push_back(nb_);
}

int main()
{
    // create 3 threads
    std::thread thread1(pushBack, 1);
    std::thread thread2(pushBack, 2);
    std::thread thread3(pushBack, 3);

    // main thread: wait until all threads are finished
    thread1.join();
    thread2.join();
    thread3.join();

    return 0;
}
```

If we remove the lock,

```cpp
    // lock mutex
    //std::lock_guard<std::mutex> lock(mutex);
```

this could happen:

```
Exception thrown at 0x7742E26F (ntdll.dll) in C11Book_VS2015.exe:
0xC0000005: Access violation reading location 0x00000001.
```

## B.  Defer + try_lock

If you try to lock a mutex already locked, the thread will wait until the mutex can be acquired, i.e. the mutex is unlocked by the other thread. You could be interested to do "something else" instead of waiting. The method is to defer the lock and use a try_lock

```cpp
#include <mutex>

std::vector<int> vec_shared;
std::mutex mutex;

void function_tryLock()
{
    // lock mutex
    std::unique_lock<std::mutex> lock(mutex, std::defer_lock);

    // try to lock mutex
    if (lock.try_lock())
    {
        vec_shared.push_back(100);
    }
    else
    {
        // do something else
    }
}
```

# 48. Concurrency: Multithread condition variables

A condition_variable is used to block a thread until another thread send a notification. It is used if you want to specify the order of the thread, otherwise a simple mutex works. The principle is:

- The thread 1 locks the mutex
- The thread 1 send this lock to the condition_variable which releases the lock and put this thread 1 in a state "wait for notification"
- The thread 2 locks the mutex
- The thread 2 manipulates the shared memory
- The thread 2 unlock the mutex (important)
- The thread 2 send the notification
- The thread 1 receive the notification + the lock
- The thread 1 manipulates the shared memory
- The thread 1 unlock and send the notification

## A. Simple example

An example with comments (without spurious wakeup check):

```cpp
#include <iostream>
#include <vector>
#include <memory>
#include <thread>
#include <mutex>

std::vector<int> vec_shared;
std::mutex mutex;
std::condition_variable conditionVariable;

void pushBack_waitForNotification(int nb_)
{
    // lock mutex
    std::unique_lock<std::mutex> lock(mutex);

    // unlock mutex and wait for notification
    std::cout << nb_ << " thread. wait for notification " << std::endl;
    conditionVariable.wait(lock);

    // notification on
    std::cout << nb_ << " thread. Notification received" << std::endl;

    // operation on shared vector
    vec_shared.push_back(nb_);
```

```cpp
    // unlock mutex
    std::cout << nb_ << " thread. Unlock and send notification" << std::endl;
    lock.unlock();

    // send notification if a thread is waiting
    conditionVariable.notify_one();
}

void pushBakc_sendNotification(int nb_)
{
    // lock mutex
    std::unique_lock<std::mutex> lock(mutex);
    std::cout << nb_ << " thread. get lock and push back" << std::endl;

    // operation on shared vector
    vec_shared.push_back(nb_);

    // unlock mutex and send notification
    std::cout << nb_ << " thread. Unlock and send notification" << std::endl;
    lock.unlock();
    conditionVariable.notify_one();
}

int main()
{
    // create thread 1 and wait for notification inside the function
    std::thread thread1(pushBack_waitForNotification, 1);

    // wait one second that the thread 1 has reached the wait for notification
    std::this_thread::sleep_for(std::chrono::seconds(1));

    // create thread 2 wich will send the notification to restart thread 1
    std::thread thread2(pushBakc_sendNotification, 2);

    // main thread: wait until all threads are finished
    thread1.join();
    thread2.join();

    // print result shared vector
    std::cout << std::endl << "vector: " << std::endl;
    for(int val: vec_shared)
        std::cout << val << std::endl;

    return 0;
}
```

And the output is:

```
1 thread. wait for notification
2 thread. get lock and push back
2 thread. Unlock and send notification
1 thread. Notification received
1 thread. Unlock and send notification

vector:
2
1
```

## B. Spurious wakeup

It is possible that the thread 1 waiting for notification will be awaken without notification from thread 2. This is due to an optimization by the library and operating system. Without this optimization the threads mechanism would be too slow. We have therefore to check if the thread 1 is indeed finished. For it we can add a lambda to the wait of the *condition_variable*:

First define a *bool done*:

```cpp
std::condition_variable conditionVariable;
bool done = false;
```

Then change the wait(…) in *pushBack_waitForNotification* function:

```cpp
conditionVariable.wait(lock, [] {return done; });
```

and set up this flag in *pushBakc_sendNotification* function:

```cpp
done = true;
lock.unlock();
conditionVariable.notify_one();
```

The full program is then:

```cpp
#include <iostream>
#include <vector>
#include <memory>
#include <thread>
#include <mutex>
#include <chrono>

std::vector<int> vec_shared;
std::mutex mutex;
std::condition_variable conditionVariable;
bool done = false;

void pushBack_waitForNotification(int nb_)
{
    // lock mutex
```

48. Concurrency: Multithread condition variables

```cpp
    std::unique_lock<std::mutex> lock(mutex);

    // unlock mutex and wait for notification
    std::cout << nb_ << " thread. wait for notification " << std::endl;
    conditionVariable.wait(lock, [] {return done; });

    // notification on
    std::cout << nb_ << " thread. Notification received" << std::endl;

    // operation on shared vector
    vec_shared.push_back(nb_);

    // unlock mutex
    std::cout << nb_ << " thread. Unlock and send notification" << std::endl;
    lock.unlock();

    // send notification if a thread is waiting
    conditionVariable.notify_one();
}

void pushBakc_sendNotification(int nb_)
{
    // lock mutex
    std::unique_lock<std::mutex> lock(mutex);
    std::cout << nb_ << " thread. get lock and push back" << std::endl;

    // operation on shared vector
    vec_shared.push_back(nb_);

    // unlock mutex and send notification
    std::cout << nb_ << " thread. Unlock and send notification" << std::endl;
    done = true;
    lock.unlock();
    conditionVariable.notify_one();
}

int main()
{
    // create thread 1 and wait for notification inside the function
    std::thread thread1(pushBack_waitForNotification, 1);

    // wait one second that the thread 1 has reached the wait for notification
    std::this_thread::sleep_for(std::chrono::seconds(1));

    // create thread 2 wich will send the notification to restart thread 1
    std::thread thread2(pushBakc_sendNotification, 2);

    // main thread: wait until all threads are finished
    thread1.join();
```

```cpp
        thread2.join();

        // print result shared vector
        std::cout << std::endl << "vector: " << std::endl;
        for(int val: vec_shared)
            std::cout << val << std::endl;

        return 0;
}
```

# 49. Index

## A

algorithm
    std::all_of, 71
    std::any_of, 71
    std::copy_if, 73
    std::count, 72
    std::count_if, 72
    std::find, 73
    std::find_if, 73
    std::for_each, 46
    std::generate, 74
    std::iota, 74
    std::is_sorted, 72
    std::max, 71
    std::min, 71
    std::minmax_element, 71
    std::none_of, 71
    std::transform, 75
alias, 14
all_of, 71
any_of, 71
array, 36
async, 78, 79
atomic, 81
attribute, 70
auto, 10

## B

bind, 76
    placeholders, 48

## C

char
    raw string literals, 9
chrono
    duration_cast, 62
    high_resolution_clock, 62
    microseconds, 62
    milliseconds, 62
    steady_clock, 62
    system_clock, 62
class
    default (function), 16
    delegating constructor, 18
    delete (function), 15, 27
    final (function), 15
    forward constructor, 19
    function keywords, 15
    inherited constructor, 19
    initialize, 8
    member initialization, 6
    override (function), 16
concurrency
    multitasks, 78
    multithread, 81, 83, 85, 87
    spurious wakeup, 87
    std::async, 78
    std::atomic, 81
    std::condition_variable, 85
    std::mutex, 83
condition_variable, 85
    spurious wakeup, 87
constexpr, 68
constructor
    delegating, 18
    forward, 19
    inherited, 19
copy_if, 73
count, 72
count_if, 72
cstdint, 56
current_exception(), 60
custom deleter, 49, 50

## D

data member initializer, 6
decltype, 11
default (function), 16
default_random_engine, 64
defer_lock, 84
deferred, 79
delegating constructor, 18
delete (function), 15, 27
duration_cast, 62

## E

emplace

vector and map, 35
enum, 53
exception_ptr, 60
exceptions, 60
external template, 41

# F

final (function), 15
find, 73
find_if, 73
for_each, 46
forward, 30, 33
forward constructor, 19
forwarding, 30
function<...>, 48

# G

generate, 74

# H

hash, 37
    std::unordered_map, 37
    std::unordered_multimap, 37
    std::unordered_multiset, 37
    std::unordered_set, 37
Hash
    hash function, 38
hash function, 38
high_resolution_clock, 62

# I

inherited constructor, 19
Initializer list, 7
int16_t, 56
int32_t, 56
int64_t, 56
int8_t, 56
iota, 74
is_sorted, 72

# L

lambda, 45
    external variable, 45
    in std::algorithm, 46
launch::async, 79
launch::deferred, 79

lock_guard, 83
long long, 54
lvalue, 21, 22, 30, 31, 33

# M

make_shared, 49
map
    emplace, 35
    initialize, 7
microseconds, 62
milliseconds, 62
min, 71
minmax_element, 71
move, 22, 33, 50
move assignement operator, 23, 28
move assignment operator, 26
move constructor, 23, 26, 28
move semantics
    lvalue, 21, 22, 30, 31, 33
    move assignement operator, 23, 28
    move assignment operator, 26
    move constructor, 23, 26, 28
    rvalue, 21, 22, 24, 30, 31, 33
    std::forward, 30, 33
    std::move, 22, 25, 33
    template, 31, 33
multitasks, 78
mutex, 83, 85
    condition_variable, 85
    std::lock_guard, 83
    std::unique_lock, 85
    try_lock, 84

# N

*noexcept*, 60
none_of, 71
normal _distribution, 64
nullptr, 43

# O

override (function), 16

# P

perfect forwarding, 30
pimpl, 50
placeholders, 48, 76

## R

R(...), 9
random generator, 64
    std:: normal_distribution, 64
    std::default_random_engine, 64
    std::uniform_int_distribution, 64
range for, 13
raw string literals, 9
regex, 65
regex_search, 65
regular expressions, 65
remove_reference, 34
rvalue, 21, 22, 24, 30, 31, 33

## S

shared_ptr, 49
    custom deleter, 49
sizeof, 54
sleep
    sleep_for, 62
sleep_for, 62
smart pointers
    std::make_shared, 49
    std::shared_ptr, 49
    std::unique_ptr, 50
    std::weak_ptr, 52
spurious wakeup, 87
static_assert, 58
static_cast, 53
std
        unique_ptr
            custom deleter, 50
std:: regex_search, 65
std:: uniform_int_distribution, 64
std::algorithm
    std::all_of, 71
    std::any_of, 71
    std::copy_if, 73
    std::count, 72
    std::count_if, 72
    std::find, 73
    std::find_if, 73
    std::for_each, 46
    std::generate, 74
    std::iota, 74
    std::is_sorted, 72
    std::max, 71
    std::min, 71
    std::minmax_element, 71

std::none_of, 71
std::transform, 75
std::all_of, 71
std::any_of, 71
std::array, 36
std::async, 78
std::atomic, 81
std::bind, 76
    placeholders, 48
std::chrono
    duration_cast, 62
    high_resolution_clock, 62
    microseconds, 62
    milliseconds, 62
    steady_clock, 62
    system_clock, 62
std::condition_variable, 85
std::copy_if, 73
std::count, 72
std::count_if, 72
std::current_exception(), 60
std::default_random_engine, 64
std::defer_lock, 84
std::exception_ptr, 60
std::find, 73
std::find_if, 73
std::for_each, 46
std::forward, 30, 33
std::function<...>, 48
std::generate, 74
std::initializer_list, 7
std::iota, 74
std::is_sorted, 72
std::launch::async, 79
std::launch::deferred, 79
std::lock_guard, 83
std::make_shared, 49
std::map
    emplace, 35
    initialize, 7
std::minmax_element, 71
std::move, 22, 33, 50
std::mutex, 83, 85
    condition_variable, 85
    std::lock_guard, 83
    std::unique_lock, 85
    try_lock, 84
std::none_of, 71
std::normal _distribution, 64
std::placeholders, 48, 76
std::regex, 65

std::shared_ptr, 49
std::this_thread
   sleep_for, 62
std::thread, 83
   condition_variable, 85
   join, 83
*std::tie*, 40
std::transform, 75
std::tuple, 40
std::unique_lock, 85
std::unique_ptr, 50
std::unordered_map, 37
std::unordered_multimap, 37
std::unordered_multiset, 37
std::unordered_set, 37
std::vector
   emplace, 35
   initialize, 7
   range for, 13
std::weak_ptr, 52
std:\max, 71
std:\min, 71
steady_clock, 62
string
   raw string literals, 9
system_clock, 62

# T

template, 31, 33
   auto, 11
   decltype, 11
   external, 41
this_thread
   sleep_for, 62
thread, 83, 85
   condition_variable, 85
   condition_variable and spurious wakeup, 87
   join, 83
   sleep_for, 62

std::lock_guard, 83
std::this_thread, 62
std::unique_lock, 85
*throw*, 60
time utilities, 62
transform, 75
tuple, 40
typedef, 14

# U

uint16_t, 56
uint32_t, 56
uint64_t, 56
uint8_t, 56
uniform_int_distribution, 64
union, 69
unique_lock, 85
unique_ptr, 50
unordered_map, 37
unordered_multimap, 37
unordered_multiset, 37
unordered_set, 37
User-defined literals, 67
using, 14

# V

variadic template, 59
vector
   emplace, 35
   initialize, 7
   range for, 13

# W

wait
   sleep_for, 62
weak_ptr, 52

Printed in Great Britain
by Amazon